ELEMENTARY METH
FOR THE
BALALAIKA

(IN FOUR PARTS—1964 REVISED EDITION)

PART I — Preparatory (Fundamentals of the Balalaika)

PART II — 1st Position—Exercises on Various Strings

PART III — 2nd, 3rd, 4th Position

PART IV — 5th, 6th, 7th, 8th Position and Supplement

BY
ALEXANDER DOROZHKIN

TRANSLATED FROM RUSSIAN BY
SIMEON N. JURIST

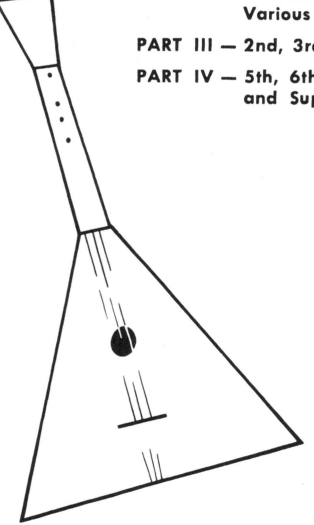

EDITED BY
DANNY HURD

THE AUTHOR'S PREFACE

The balalaika is one of the most popular musical instruments of the Soviet Union. It is played not only by Russians, but also by people of numerous other nationalities inhabiting the U.S.S.R. Instructions on how to play the balalaika are given at all levels of Soviet musical education. A great number of balalaika instruction books, methodologies, research studies and repertories were published in that country for numerous balalaika fans.

This attention to a rather modest, three-string musical instrument can be explained by the fact that the balalaika is a fully accomplished modern musical tool whose chromatic sound arrangement brings out the brightest possibilities for artistic expression possessed only by the balalaika. Some of the oustanding contemporary artists of the U.S.S.R. like State Laureate P. Necheporenko, laureates of International Competitions N. Nekrasov and A. Tikhonov, as well as many others include in their repertories not only original compositions written specifically for the balalaika, but also transcriptions of some of the greatest works of Tschaikovsky, Glinka, Liszt, Mozart and of the contemporary Soviet and other composers.

Balalaika became a full fledged member of the orchestras of some of the best Soviet ensembles like Alexandrov's Red Bannered ensemble of song and dance of the Soviet army, the Moyseyev ensemble, Berezka etc.

Balalaika plays an outstanding role in national people's orchestras of the U.S.S.R., in Osipov's state's people's orchestra, in the Folk Instruments Orchestra of the Central Radio and Television, in the Folk Instruments Orchestra of the Leningrad Radio and others.

In addition to that, virtually thousands of collectives of amateurs, whose musical accomplishments often rival those of professional orchestras devote themselves to the art of balalaika.

The present instruction book has been written for amateur musicians who are balalaika fans. It is intended to serve as a self-taught course for acquiring preliminary habits and techniques of playing the balalaika.

The instruction book consists of four parts.

The first part—Preparatory—acquaints the potential player with preliminary information about this instrument, with music and fundamentals of balalaika technique, indicating the positioning of the thumb and index finger of the left hand and the simplest usage of the fingers of the right hand for purposes of producing balalaika sounds.

The second part is devoted to the detailed study of methods of playing in the first position. This part also deals with new information pertaining to the theory of music, so essential for practical studies.

The third part acquaints the reader with the study of the second, third and fourth positions. The concluding section of this part contains musical pieces strengthening the digestion of previously acquired material.

The fourth part—Supplement—contains a repertory in which all the fundamental eight positions are used.

Considering the specific characteristics of the instrument the instruction book contains a small glossary of technical terms.

The repertory of this work is made up of Russian, Ukrainian, Byelorussian and Czech folksongs, popular works of contemporary Soviet composers and of pieces by the founders of virtuoso balalaika playing, V. V. Andreyev and B. S. Troyanovsky.

The author hopes that this book will assist the American music lovers in mastering the technique of playing the popular Soviet musical instrument balalaika in realization that the performance of Soviet music and of folk songs of the U.S.S.R. will unquestionably contribute to the improvement of understanding between our peoples.

All wishes and comments pertaining to this studybook will be greatly welcomed and appreciated by the author.

Wishing you every success,

A. DOROZHKIN

U.S.S.R. Moscow January, 1963

ALEXANDER DOROZHKIN

A. TIHONOV, virtuoso,
soloist with Russian People's Orchestra

RUSSIAN PEOPLE'S ORCHESTRA
of Moscow Subway Workers and Builders

V

UNITED RUSSIAN PEOPLE'S ORCHESTRA
With Representatives of Various Regions of U.S.S.R.

TABLE OF CONTENTS

PART I - PREPARATORY

CHAPTER I

A brief explanation about the instrument

The balalaika is a stringed Russian folk instrument. Its wide-spread use in Russia dates back to the first half of the eighteenth century. In the latter part of the nineteenth century V. V. Andreyev in collaboration with the master instrument maker F. Passerbsky reconstructed the balalaika. The finger-board was improved by incorporating metal frets placed in chromatic order. A permanent tuning was adopted. Mechanical tuning pegs were introduced. Gut strings, producing a soft chesty sound, became popular and the body of the instrument was given a beautiful triangular shape. S. I. Nalimov and other master craftsmen began to produce instruments of high concert quality.

The improved balalaika acquired wide popularity. Side by side with amateurs there appeared soloists-virtuosi such as V. Andreyev and B. S. Troyanovsky who by their brilliant performances created great respect for the instrument both at home and abroad.

By the end of the nineteenth century and the beginning of the twentieth further development of the balalaika art led to the organization of many balalaika -player groups and, with the reconstruction of the domra[1] and the psaltery,[2] to the establishment of a Russian National Folk Instrument Orchestra.

Choosing, care and handling of the Balalaika

When acquiring a balalaika the following must be observed: (1) the fingerboard must be straight; (2) the frets must be carefully rounded and polished; (3) the height of the strings above the twelfth fret not more than 3 to 4 mm. (approximately 1/8"); (4) strings must sound clear and melodious on all frets without any buzzing; (5) the tuning mechanism must work easily and smoothly; (6) the external appearance of the instrument must be attractive and without any defects in the polish or finish.

The instrument should be kept in a cover or case to protect it from heat, cold and moisture. After playing wipe the fingerboard and strings carefully with a soft rag.

When restringing the instrument try to keep the new strings properly tuned. All necessary repairs, such as change of frets, glueing, etc., should be done by a specialist.

Preparing the instrument for practice

STRINGING. Metal, gut or nylon strings can be used on balalaikas. The first string, of .28 to .30 mm. thickness,[3] is always made of metal. The other two, .90 to 1.00 mm. thick, are most frequently made of gut or nylon. To string the instrument, placed the looped end of the string over the head of the button (see Fig. 1), then pull the string over the lower ridge, bridge and upper ridge to the peg. Wind the string a couple of times over the stem of the peg (Fig. 2), then once through the hole in the peg (Fig. 3) and finally wind the end twice over the string itself (Fig. 4). After that tighten the string by turning the peg.

LOCATION OF THE BRIDGE. Factory-made instruments usually have a special mark on the sounding board to indicate the placement of the bridge. However, if there is no such mark, the player can easily locate the precise place. Simply measure the distance from the upper ridge to the 12th fret, then measure an equal distance down from the 12th fret and make a mark on the sounding-board. This is where the bridge is to be placed (Fig. 1). The bridge must fit smoothly on the surface of the sounding-board.

---

1 Russian stringed instrument of the lute family.
2 Ancient stringed instrument of zither family.
3 It is not always possible to obtain readily strings made expressly for the balalaika, in which case substitute strings of the proper length and tension can usually be found. (Length may vary with the individual instrument; desirable tension depends on the player's personal preference or muscular development.) Reasonable substitutes include a tenor banjo A string and gut or nylon classic guitar E strings. - The editor

2

DIAGRAM OF
A BALALAIKA

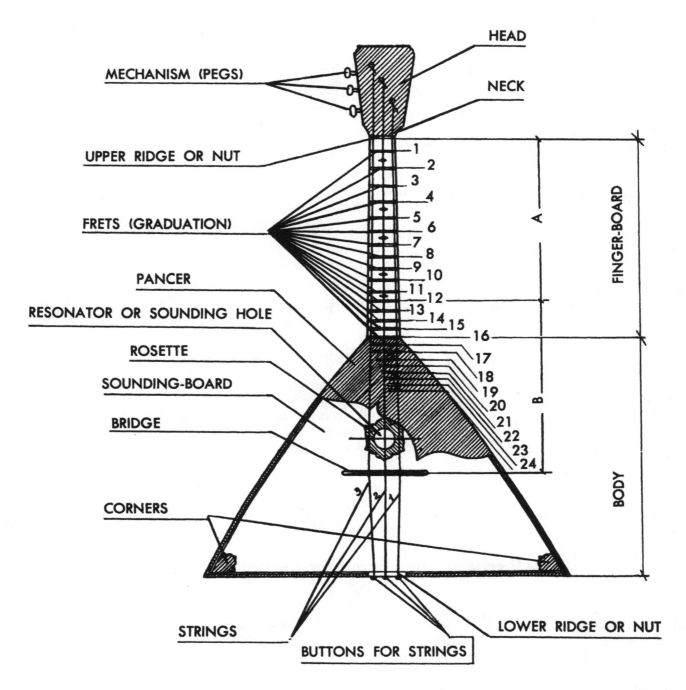

MECHANISM (PEGS)

HEAD

NECK

UPPER RIDGE OR NUT

FRETS (GRADUATION)

PANCER

RESONATOR OR SOUNDING HOLE

ROSETTE

SOUNDING-BOARD

BRIDGE

CORNERS

STRINGS

BUTTONS FOR STRINGS

FINGER-BOARD

A

B

BODY

LOWER RIDGE OR NUT

A—DISTANCE FROM UPPER RIDGE TO 12th FRET

B—DISTANCE FROM THE 12th FRET TO BRIDGE

FIG. 1

FIG. 2

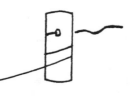

FIG. 3

FIG. 4

TUNING OF THE INSTRUMENT. The tuning is started with the first string,[1] the sound of which must correspond to the sound A of the first octave (a') played on bayan, accordion or piano.   This sound is also produced by the first (thin)(E) string of a guitar pressed down on the fifth fret or by the second open string of a mandolin or domra.

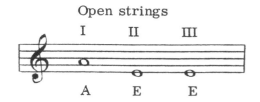

Open strings

After that the second and third strings are tuned in unison, the sound of each pressed down on the 5th fret being the same as the open first string (A).   Shown above is the notation on the staff of the sounds of the open strings when the instrument is properly tuned.

As may be seen from the above notation example, the sound of the first string (A) is indicated by a note placed in the second space of the staff. The note E (sound of second and third strings) is written on the first line.

Order of daily practice

1. Playing of scales and exercises by different strokes and manners of playing. . 5 to 15 minutes
2. Work on etudes to secure the habit of using various positions, manners of playing and strokes . . . . 10 to 20 minutes
3. Work on new pieces . . . . 40 to 60 minutes
4. Playing from memory and perfecting execution of pieces learned earlier. . . 35 to 55 minutes

1-1/2 to 2-1/2 hours

Correct sitting position

The balalaika player should sit on the forward part of a straight chair, lower legs straight and knees slightly spread.   Move the right leg back a little and place the corner of the instrument between the knees,   pressing it lightly with the right elbow toward the body.   The finger-board is held between the thumb and the index finger of the left hand.

Notation of musical sounds

Musical sounds (tones) are expressed on paper by notes.[2] Notes express both duration and pitch. Duration is indicated as follows:

These are four quarter-notes. The oval head is black (filled in) and the stem is on the right side going up from the head or on the left side going down.   A quarter note gets one beat.

These are two half notes. The oval head is empty.   A half note is twice as long as a quarter, or two beats.

This is a whole note and is equivalent to four quarters or two halves (four beats).

---

1 (Note position of strings 3, 2, 1 in Fig. 1)
2 Editor's note: Strictly speaking tones (or sounds) are what we hear and notes are what we see. The two terms are often loosely interchanged.

4

Each exercise or piece is divided by straight vertical lines called bars (or bar lines) into segments called measures (or bars) in which the sum total of note values (durations) corresponds with the meter of the piece as indicated by the time signature.

The time signature consists of the two numbers at the beginning of each composition, for example, $\frac{3}{4}$ $\frac{4}{4}$ $\frac{2}{4}$. The upper figure show the number of beats in a measure and the lower figure indicates what kind of a note gets one beat. ($\frac{3}{4}$ means there are three beats in a measure and a quarter note gets one beat.)

At the very beginning of a piece or exercise written for balalaika appears the treble clef, or G clef: Most instrumental and vocal music is written with this clef and notes are located on the staff in the following manner:

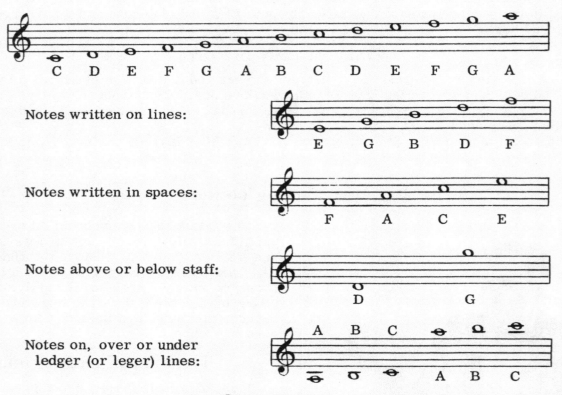

C D E F G A B C D E F G A

Notes written on lines:

E G B D F

Notes written in spaces:

F A C E

Notes above or below staff:

D G

Notes on, over or under ledger (or leger) lines:

A B C A B C

Open strings

Several different methods of sound production are used in playing the balalaika, to provide a wide range of expression or interpretation of various compositions.

One of these manners of playing is arpeggiato, a down stroke with the right thumb.[1] Arpeggiato is indicated by a wavy vertical line before the notes.

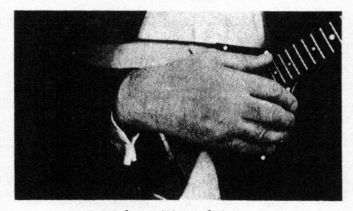

Initial position of the wrist

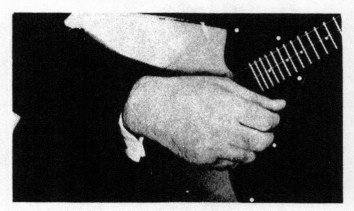

Terminal position of the wrist

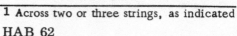

1 Across two or three strings, as indicated

Exercises which are necessary for mastering the technique of playing by the arpeggiato method must be repeated several times. Counting in $\frac{4}{4}$ time - "one, two, three, four" - each count represents one beat. A quarter note (♩) gets one beat. A half note (♩) is sustained for two beats, and a whole note (o) is sustained for four beats. Thus, in Exercise ☐1 on open strings there are four separate strokes in each measure, one on each count. In Exercise ☐2 there are only two strokes in each measure, one on count "one" (sustain for count "two") and another on count "three" (sustain for "four"). Exercise ☐3 has one stroke to the measure, on the first beat (count "one"), sustaining for "two, three, four". It is important to count rhythmically, evenly and without interruption, every beat of the exercises when practicing.

These indicate that all music between the (repeat) signs must be played twice. (If only the sign on the right appears, the composition must be repeated from the beginning.)

While playing the "Exercises on open strings" and the song "Andrew" it is necessary to watch for a correct sitting position and the placement of the hands. The strings must be stroked lightly, producing a clear and pleasant sound. Counting may be done aloud or mentally.

For the convenience of the student in Part I and Part II of this book under each staff will be found a diagram of three lines, representing the three strings of the instrument. The upper line represents the A string, the middle and lower lines the two E strings. Note heads on any of these three lines indicate open strings and numerals refer to frets.

Exercises on open strings

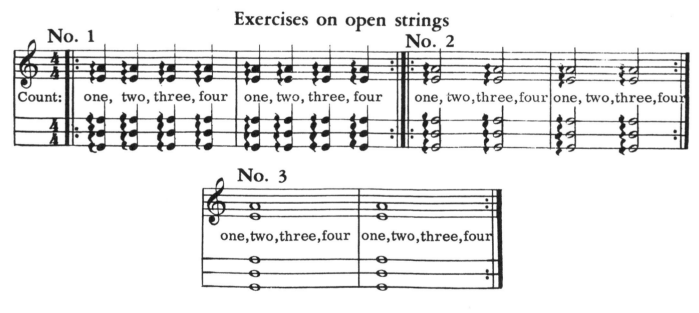

1. ANDREW

A Russian story-teller's exordium

6

CHAPTER II

Placement of the first and second fingers of the left hand

The shortest distance (or interval) between two musical sounds in our system is a half-step (also called half-tone or semitone). For example, the interval between the sounds played on any two adjacent frets of the same string (2nd and 3rd frets, 5th and 6th frets, 1st fret and open) is a half-step. An interval of two half-steps is a whole-step (whole-tone).

After the notes E and A (the open strings) the pupil must learn the location of notes B and C. The note B is written on the third line of the staff and the note C is written in the third space (between the third and fourth lines). Between notes A and B there is an interval of a whole-step, so the sound B is produced by pressing the A string on the second fret. Between the notes B and C the interval is a half-step, so C is produced by pressing the A string on the third fret.

When producing the sounds B and C the fingers must be placed steeply and firmly on the string at the proper fret of the finger-board. Use the first (index) finger for B, the second finger for C.

The following exercise is played entirely on the A string, using a down stroke of the right thumb. This manner of playing is called pizzicato (plucking).

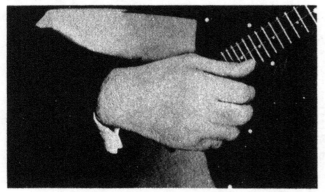

Initial position of the thumb

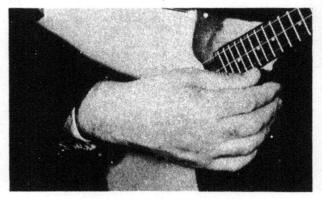

Terminal position of the thumb

In the following exercises and pieces, be sure to give exact time values to quarter and half notes. Avoid buzzing or clanking sounds; strive for clear, beautiful sounds.

Position of B and C on the A string

Exercises for developing the first and second fingers of the left hand

The count of beats and fingering for the following pieces should be indicated by the student.

2. MELODY

A. DOROZHKIN

3. IN THE GARDEN A HARE IS RUNNING

RUSSIAN FOLK SONG

The strumming style of playing

Strumming is the basic style of balalaika playing. This manner of playing consists of down and up strokes by the index finger of the right hand. To attain a soft, clear sound the strings must be struck near the finger-board by the flesh of the finger (not by the finger-nail). The right wrist must move freely, without any tension.

HAB 62

8

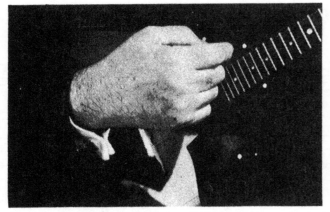
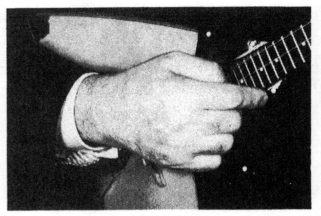

Initial position of the wrist   Terminal position of the wrist

Exercises for developing the technique of strumming must be played on all strings. The first and second fingers of the left hand should be positioned on the A string while the E strings remain open.

Play each exercise several times, then try to commit to memory the pieces, striving always to attain a smooth, unhampered execution. Notice the symbols indicating direction of index-finger strokes: ⊓ down stroke; V up stroke.

Exercises

4. IN THE GARDEN

RUSSIAN FOLK SONG

Placement of the left thumb

The sounds F and G are produced on the E strings. Note F is located in the first space of the staff (between the first and second lines) and note G is on the second line. The interval between E and F is a half-step; between F and G there is a whole-step. To produce the sound F both E strings must be pressed down at the first fret by the left thumb. To obtain the sound G the E strings must be pressed down by the thumb at the third fret. The strings must be pressed down firmly in order to produce a pure, clear sound.

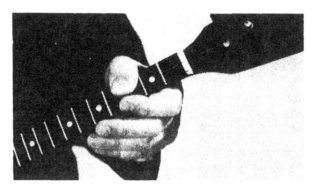

The right thumb is used in the following exercises to strike the second and third (E) strings (arpeggiato). After gliding over the two E strings the right thumb must stop at the A string, then take its initial position again over the third string. Do not play loud. Rather, strive to achieve a beautiful, soft sound.

Location of notes F and G on the E strings

Exercises for developing the left thumb

No.1

No. 2

The following song ("As Our Girl-Friends Went") begins on the third beat. The first measure has fewer beats than the time signature indicates and is considered irregular. In accordance with this, the last measure will have as many beats as were missing in the first measure.[1] The song begins with the count "three".

5. AS OUR GIRL-FRIENDS WENT

RUSSIAN FOLK SONG

Exercises for developing the fingers of the left hand while playing on all strings

No.1

No. 2

1 Editor's note - This rule regarding the final measure is not strictly observed today.

Symbols for raising and lowering basic sounds

Basic sounds — C, D, E, F, G, A, B — can be raised or lowered when necessary.   For this purpose there are special alteration symbols —— sharps and flats.

A sharp (♯) before a note raises it a half-step.
A flat (♭) before a note lowers it a half-step.

For example, the note C on the A string is played on the third fret, but a sharp placed before it raises it a half-step and it must be played on the fourth fret (C♯).

The note B on the A string is played on the second fret, but the same note with a flat before it becomes B♭ and is to be played a half-step lower, on the first fret.

If a note which has been raised or lowered is to be restored to its original sound a natural (♮) is placed before it.

Sharps or flats may belong to the key of a piece or they may be accidental. When sharps or flats are grouped in a key signature (following the clef on the staff) they are effective throughout the piece. Accidentals (sharps, flats or naturals appearing anywhere but in the key signature) are effective only in the measure where they occur.

Exercises 3 and 4 and pieces 6 through 9 all have a key signature of one sharp. Every written F is automatically F♯, played on the second fret of both E strings.

Exercises

No. 3

No. 4

6. ETUDE

A. DOROZHKIN

7. MELODY

A. DOROZHKIN

8. FOLK MELODY

A. DOROZHKIN

9. IN THE ORCHARD BY THE GARDEN

RUSSIAN FOLK SONG

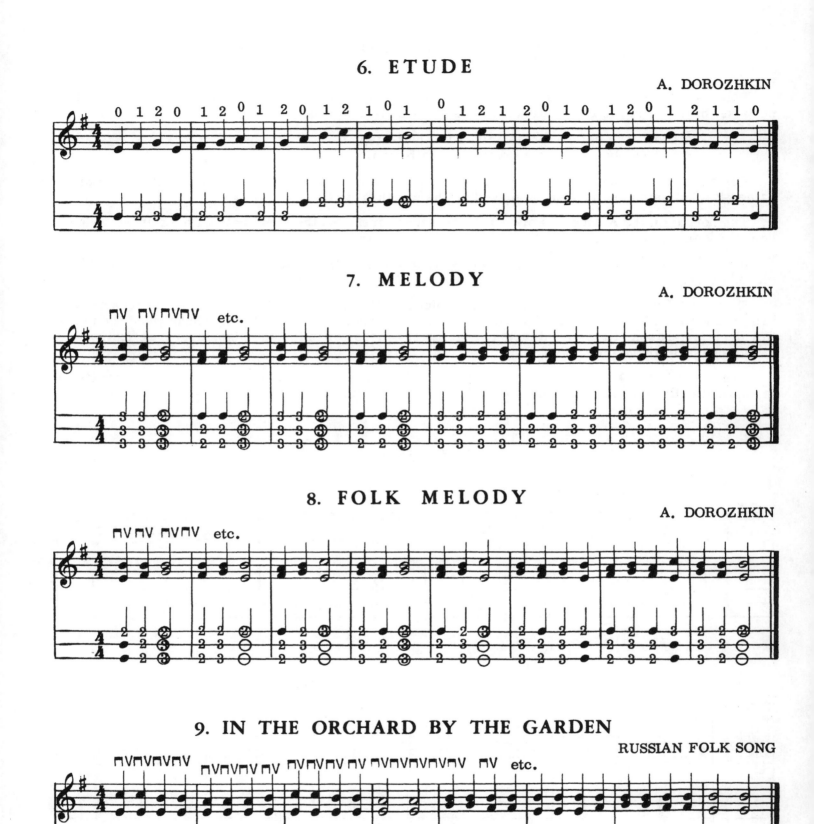

PART II

CHAPTER III
FIRST POSITION

Sound range and placement of the fingers of the left hand in first position

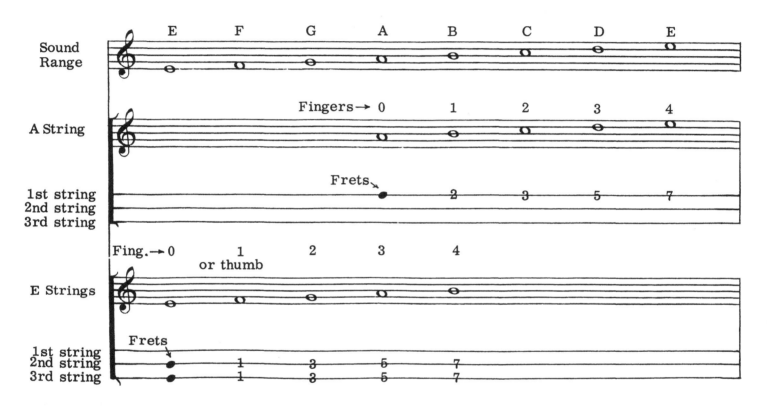

Basic sounds (notes) C, D, E, F, G, A, B repeat in sequence and embrace all the frets of a balalaika. For convenience in referring to a specific note the continuous scale is divided into octaves.

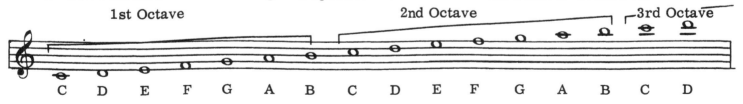

(An octave actually consists of eight notes, as from C of the first octave to C of the second octave, or from D of the second octave to D of the third octave.)

The placement of the fingers of the left hand on the fingerboard is defined by the term <u>position</u>.

<u>First position</u> encompasses notes from E of the first octave to E of the second. On the E strings the notes in first position are E, F, G, A, B. On the A string first position notes are A, B, C, D, E. Observe that notes A and B can be played on the E strings as well as on the A string. When pressing a string at the fret hold the finger steeply. When the next finger in turn is placed on the string the preceding one is not taken off the string. The third and fourth fingers of the left hand are less agile than the others and more attention must be given to developing them.

Left hand in first position on the A string

These (♫ or ♪♪) are eighth notes. Single eighth notes have a flag or hook ♪ 𝄽 . Two or more eighths may be joined by a beam ▬▬▬ . They are played twice as fast as quarter notes. To indicate eighth notes in counting, add the word "and". (Count "one and two and", etc.)

Alternating strokes of the strings by the thumb (T) and index finger (I) of the right hand constitute the <u>double plucking</u> manner of playing. The thumb plucks with a down stroke and the index finger makes an up stroke.

In the song "In the Field a Birch Tree Stood" we come across some dotted notes (dotted quarters). Such notes are held one and a half times as long as quarter notes without a dot.

A dot placed to the right of a note increases its duration by half of its time value.

$$\text{♩. } = \text{♩} + \text{♪} = \text{♪} + \text{♪} + \text{♪}$$

Exercises ①, ② and ③ and the song "On the Green Meadow" are written in the key of A, with a key signature of three sharps. Every F, every C and every G must be played a half-step higher (F♯, C♯, G♯).

At the beginning of each piece from now on you will find Italian terms which indicate the tempo or character of the piece.[1]   For example, "Allegretto" (somewhat fast), "Leggiero" (lightly). Some of the pieces have numbers in squares (①, ②). These are to help the student in locating sections of a piece when practicing.

Exercises and pieces on the A string

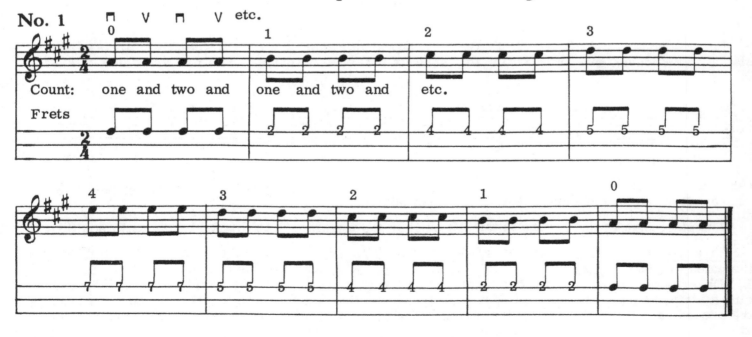

1 Meanings of Italian and other tempo, expression and playing indications can be found in a music dictionary.   It is advisable for the student to own at least a good pocket dictionary of musical terms   - Editor

Nuances, or shadings, are indicated by dynamic signs which show the relative intensity with which any given section of a piece should be played.

Each exercise is to be played several times by the double plucking method. First play it *f,* then *p* . Later repeat each exercise, diminishing the volume each time: (1) *f*, (2) *mf* , (3) *p*.Then, reverse the order: (1) *p*, (2) *mf*, (3) *f*.

No. 2

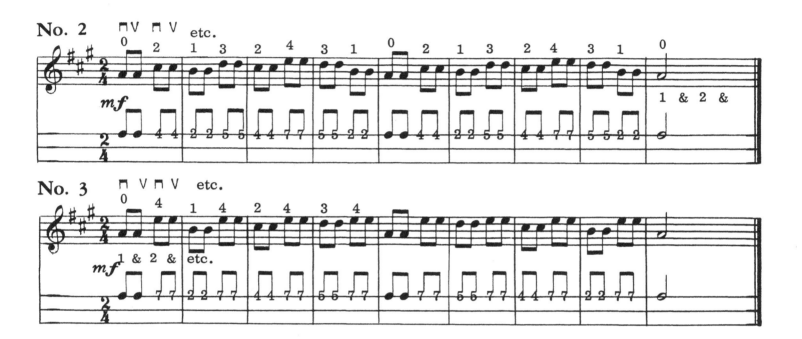

10. A MIRACLE BEYOND THE RIVER

RUSSIAN FOLK-SONG

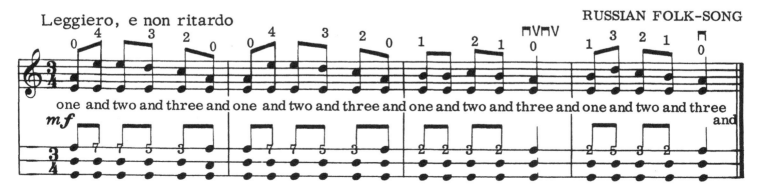

11. ON THE GREEN MEADOW

Con moto

RUSSIAN FOLK SONG

12. IN THE FIELD A BIRCH TREE STOOD

RUSSIAN FOLK SONG

Moderato

13. IN THE PINE GROVE A PATH IS WINDING

14. VISIT ME, MY FRIEND

CHAPTER IV

Exercises on the E string and pieces in first position

The following exercises (No. 1, No. 2, No. 3) are designed to give the student a variety of techniques while learning the first position on the E string(s).

The <u>left hand</u> should be used in two different ways with each of the right hand manners of playing: (1) using the <u>fingers</u> to press the strings on the frets and (2) using the <u>thumb</u>.

For developing agility of the thumb and index finger of the <u>right hand</u> Exercise No. 1 is to be played as follows:

       (1) striking with the thumb only (⊓);
       (2) striking with the index finger only (V);
       (3) alternating measures of thumb and index;
       (4) striking down with the thumb and up with the index finger
           (double plucking each note).

Manners of playing to be applied in practicing Exercise No. 1

Exercises

No. 1

No. 2

No. 3 Can be played TI (double plucking) or strumming style[1]

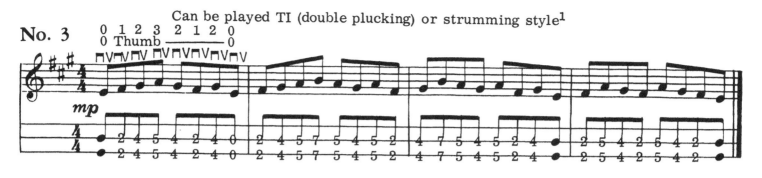

15. LITTLE POLKA

Moderato

D. KABALEVSKY

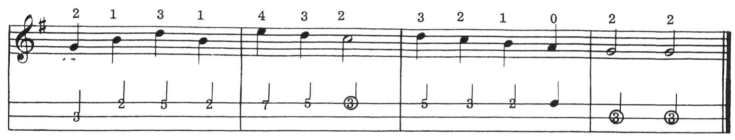

16. OVER THE LITTLE BRIDGE

Con anima

RUSSIAN FOLK-SONG

[1] When double plucking, use 2nd string only and press it against the frets with the fingers of the left hand When strumming, press 2nd and 3rd strings with left thumb and allow one or more of the fingers to deaden the A string by resting lightly against it. (Technically, the stems of notes in Exercise No. 3 should be crossed by short lines as in No. 2; however, when ⊓V is indicated over one note the repetition is automatic.

HAB 62

17. I WILL GO

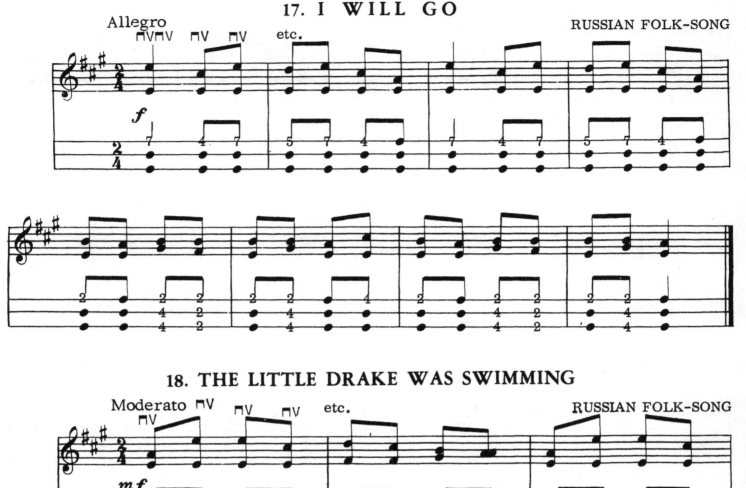

Allegro

RUSSIAN FOLK-SONG

18. THE LITTLE DRAKE WAS SWIMMING

Moderato

RUSSIAN FOLK-SONG

Signs and indicate repeat endings. (1st ending and 2nd ending). As mentioned before, the sign :|| requires that all measures following ||: (or from the beginning if there is no ||:) be repeated. The measures in the 1st ending are played the first time only. On the second playing the first ending is skipped and the second ending played instead.

19. I'LL SCATTER MY WOES

RUSSIAN FOLK-SONG

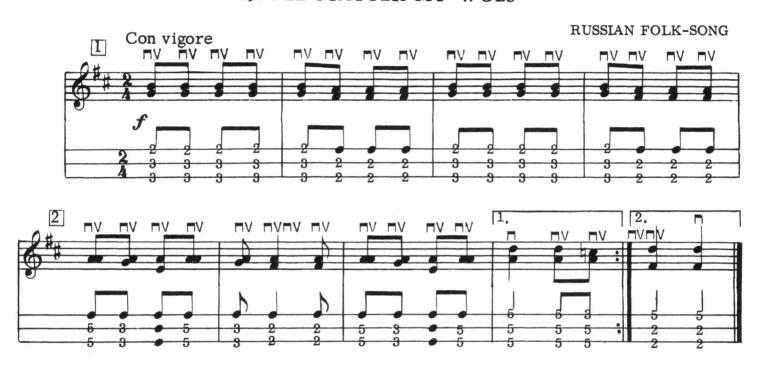

20. UKRAINIAN FOLK SONG

Arranged by D. VASSILIEV-
BUGLAI and A. DOROZHKIN

21. SHALL YOU BE TAUGHT, JOHNNY?

Allegro con moto

RUSSIAN FOLK-SONG

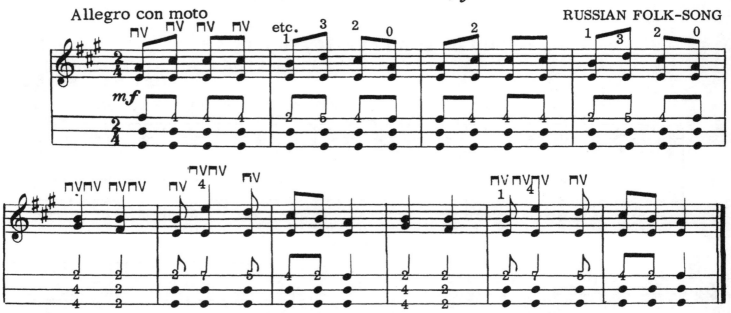

22. MY PORCH

Allegretto

RUSSIAN FOLK-SONG

CHAPTER V
SIXTEENTH NOTES

Sixteenth notes have two beams or flags. They are usually grouped by fours. Four sixteenths equal one quarter. For example,

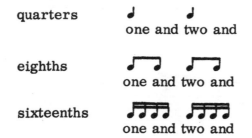

quarters

one and two and

eighths

one and two and

sixteenths

one and two and

Note that two sixteenths are played for the count "one" and the third sixteenth falls on the "and".

When playing a group of sixteenth notes the strokes by the right index finger are alternately down and up (⊓V⊓V). In mixed groups of eighth and sixteenth notes the stroking is as follows:

one and   one and

23. I DANCED WITH A MOSQUITO

RUSSIAN COMEDY FOLK SONG

24. I AM SITTING ON A ROCK

RUSSIAN FOLK ROUND

25. DOWN THE STREET[1]

Largamente

RUSSIAN FOLK-SONG

Chords

In music for the balalaika there are sometimes found combinations of three notes ——triads or chords. The thumb is used on the outside E string (3rd string) to play the lowest note of the chord and the other two notes are to be played by the left hand fingers on the upper two strings.

In "Ural Mountain Dance Song" the triad E-G♯-B can be fingered in two ways:

First method (preferred)

Second method

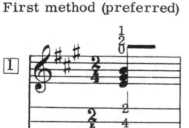

---

1 Short lines crossing stems of notes signify breaking the basic note into repeated notes, according to how many flags, beams or cross-lines there are altogether.

Examples: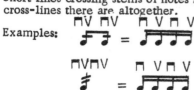

26. URAL MOUNTAIN DANCE SONG

RUSSIAN FOLK SONG
Arr. by B. TROYANOVSKY

Largamente, con Risoluzione

27. LISTEN, FELLOWS

RUSSIAN COMEDY FOLK-SONG
Arr. by A. ILIUKHIN

Con gioia

28. YOUNG MAIDEN

RUSSIAN FOLK SONG

Scherzando

29. BY OUR GATE

RUSSIAN FOLK SONG

Allegro con vigore

30. THE DITCH

Larghetto

RUSSIAN COMEDY FOLK SONG

31. ALL GODMOTHERS LEFT FOR HOME

Con anima

RUSSIAN COMEDY FOLK SONG

CHAPTER VI

TREMOLO, LEGATO, SCALES

The <u>tremolo</u> manner of playing consists of fast, evenly alternating down and up strokes by the index finger of the right hand. Tremolo playing creates an impression of continuous sound and suggests singing.

If in a piece of music there are no indications of manners of playing such as arpeggiato (⟨), pizzicato (·∨ ⊓) or double plucking (TI) and there are notes of long value (whole or half) or a number of short ones which are connected on top or below by an arched line ⌒ called a <u>slur,</u> they are to be played in the tremolo manner. The passage of music included within the slur is played "legato" (literally, "bound together"). At the end of the slur the tremolo must stop, as for a short breath (luftpause or caesura), then resume for the next slurred phrase. Use of tremolo plus "breathing" serves to phrase the music and to separate one phrase from another.

In the song "Beyond the Swift River" the time value of the second voice (lower notes) does not always coincide with that of the first (upper) voice. For instance, the note A on the E strings is to be sustained for three beats ("one and two and one and") while four different notes are played on the A string. The tremolo serves to keep the two voices in balance.

The sign ◁────── (crescendo) indicates an increase in sound intensity and the sign ──────▷ (decrescendo or diminuendo) a gradual decrease in volume.

32. BEYOND THE SWIFT RIVER

SLOW RUSSIAN FOLK SONG

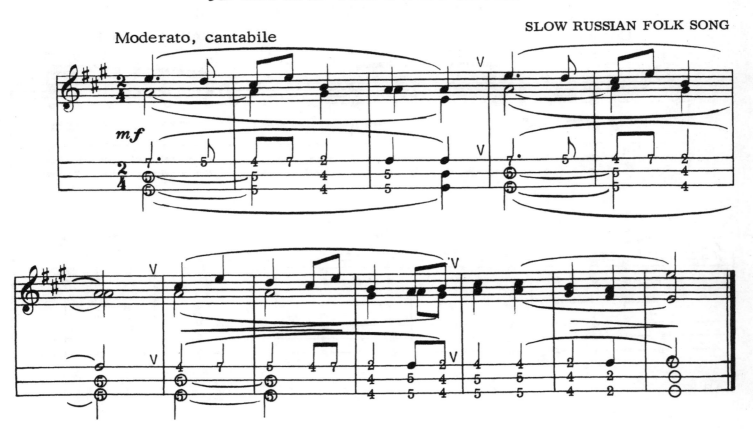

33. GLORIFICATION

Grandioso con solennità

RUSSIAN FOLK-SONG

Scales

Scales are widely used for ear training, developing agility of the fingers and study of the fingerboard and playing manners. A scale is a number of sounds placed in ascending or descending order by degrees of (whole-) steps and half-steps.

Scales are usually played from their initial sound to its octave. For instance, the C scale is played from C of the second octave to C of the third octave. The G scale can be played from G of the first octave to G of the second octave, and so on.

Major scales are built on the principle of step, step, half-step, step, step, step, half-step. (1-1-1/2-1-1-1-1/2).

For instance, the scale of C major:

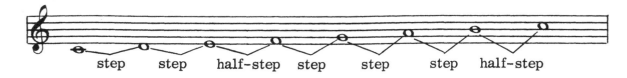

step   step   half-step   step   step   step   half-step

A major scale can be built on any note according to this principle.

Minor scales have a different structure from the major and appear in three different forms: natural, melodic and harmonic. Melodic minor scales also have different forms ascending and descending.

For example, the scale of A melodic minor:

Ascending (1-1/2-1-1-1-1-1/2)

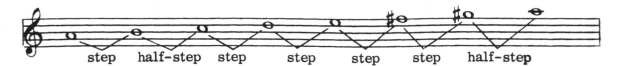

step   half-step   step   step   step   step   half-step

30

Descending (1-1-1/2-1-1-1/2-1)

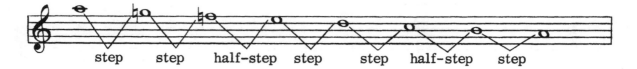

step   step   half-step   step   step   half-step   step

The natural and harmonic minor scales retain the same form ascending and descending.

A natural minor (1-1/2-1-1-1/2-1-1):

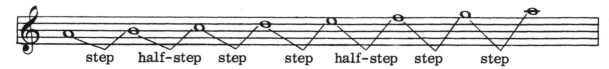

step   half-step   step   step   half-step   step   step

A harmonic minor (1-1/2-1-1-1/2-1 1/2-1/2)

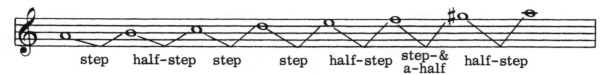

step   half-step   step   step   half-step   step-&
a-half   half-step

Memorize each scale, including the indicated fingering. It is recommended that scales be played up and down several times at the beginning of the daily practice period, in order to limber up the
fingers.

E Major Scale

E Minor Scale (melodic)

Fingering and plucking are the same for the minor as for the major scale.   Scales must be repeated several times, striving for rhythmic precision, clarity of sound and, gradually, faster tempo.

PART III

CHAPTER VII
SECOND POSITION

The second position embraces sounds from G of the first octave to F of the second. Second position sounds on the E string are G, A, B, C and on the A string C, D, E, F.

In the second position the left hand fingers are placed closer to the bridge than in the first position. The left index finger will now be on the third fret. Note that sound A in the second position must be played on the E string, 5th fret, and sound B also on the E string, 7th fret. Sound C may be played either on the E string 8th fret or the A string 3rd fret.

Stretch the fingers with confidence and press the strings firmly at the frets. When placing the next finger in turn on the string the preceding one should not be lifted. (Legato style.) Do not allow any buzzing sounds and do not play loud.

Left hand in second position

Sound range and placement of fingers in second position

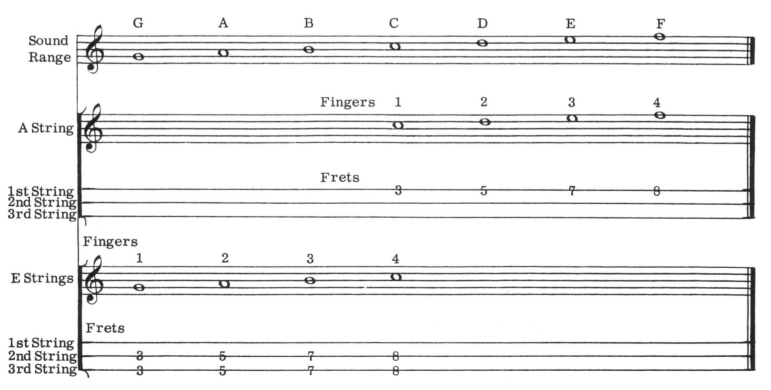

Exercises in second position

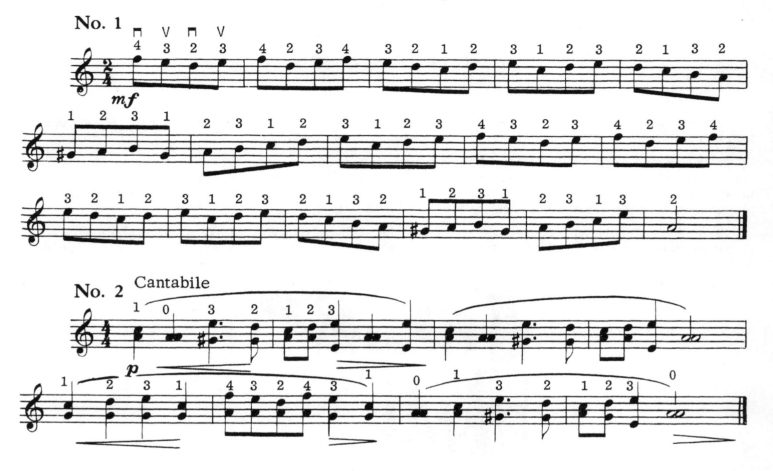

The song "Under the Apple Tree" requires familiarity with both the first and second positions. (Note, for instance, that the first measure must be played in second position, then the second measure plus the following eighth note are in first position.) Learn this song by memory to get used to playing in both positions. Play the song broadly and gaily.

Over the first chord of the song (and over the first chord of the third, fifth and seventh measures) appear the letters "Fr". This symbol calls for friser,[1] a manner of playing in which the strings are stroked downward in turn by the four fingers of the right hand, beginning with the little finger. Friser is used mostly at the beginning of lively dance melodies.

Indications concerning the movements of the right wrist (ᐯᑎ) must be strictly observed.

34. UNDER THE APPLE TREE

RUSSIAN FOLK ROUND
Arr. by P. KARKIN

1 Friser is French for "curl", is also translated "roll". See "roll" in glossary.

F Major Scale

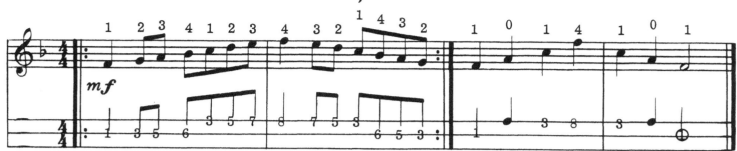

F Minor Scale (melodic)

35. DANCE SONG

Allegro

N. BUDASHKIN, Op. 17, No. 2

When stems of notes are crossed with three short slanted lines the notes are to be played tremolo style.

CHAPTER VIII
THIRD POSITION

Sounds from A of the first octave to G of the second comprise the range of the third position. Sounds on the E string are A, B, C, D and on the A string D, E, F, G.

Diligent work on exercises, scales and the Russian folk song "The Little Willow Tree" will facilitate learning well the three studied positions.

Left hand in third position

Sound range and placement of fingers in third position

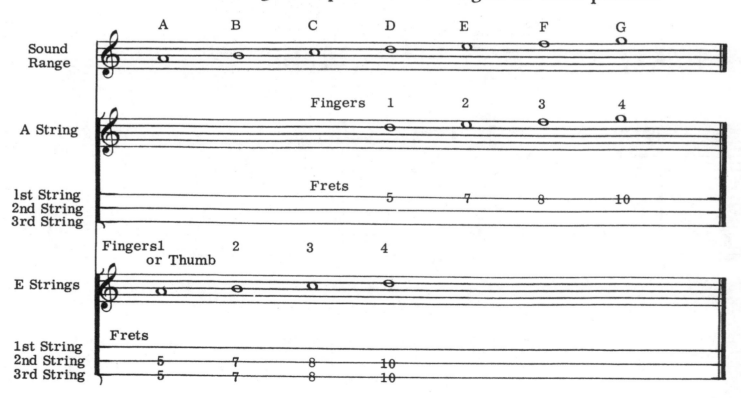

Exercises for Combining the First, Second and Third Positions

No. 1

Roman numerals under the staff indicate positions. Follow these indications. Play the exercise by the double plucking method.

No. 2 Cantabile, con sonora

Play this exercise by the tremolo method, engaging all strings.

In this song pay particular attention to the stroking as indicated.

36. THE LITTLE WILLOW TREE

Moderato con amore

RUSSIAN FOLK-SONG

G Major Scale

G Minor Scale (melodic)

HAB 62

In this song you will come across symbols 𝄾 and 𝄽 which are signs of rest or pause. They indicate the duration of silence.

𝄾 is an eighth rest, equivalent to ♪

𝄽 is a quarter rest, equivalent to ♩

37. WE WERE NOT FRIENDLY

B. MOKROUSSOV

Moderato e sostenuto

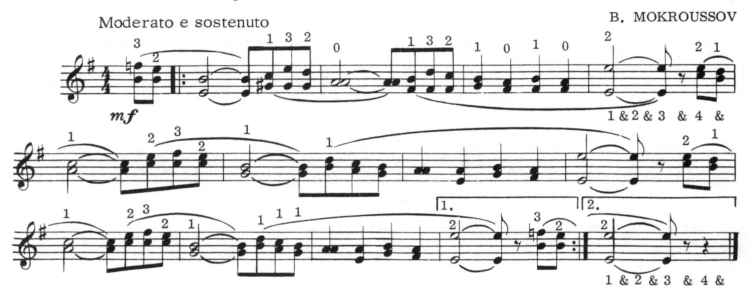

CHAPTER IX

FOURTH POSITION

Sounds from B of the first octave to A of the second comprise the range of the fourth position. Sounds on the E string are B, C, D, E and on the A string E, F, G, A. Exercises, scales and pieces help the student to become familiar with the fourth position and to combine it with the previous three positions. Work out carefully the transitions from one position to another, in order to develop fast and exact movement of the left hand on the finger-board.

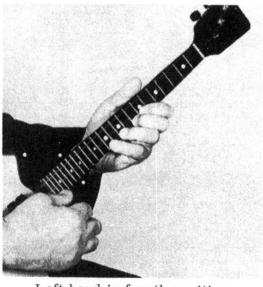

Left hand in fourth position

Sound range and placement of fingers in fourth position

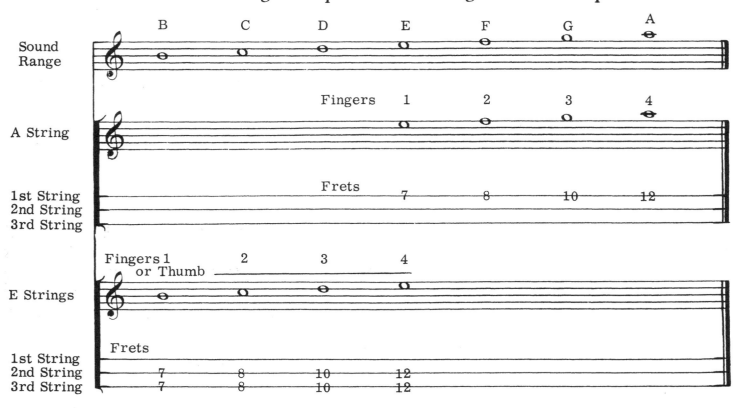

Exercises for combining the first, second and fourth positions

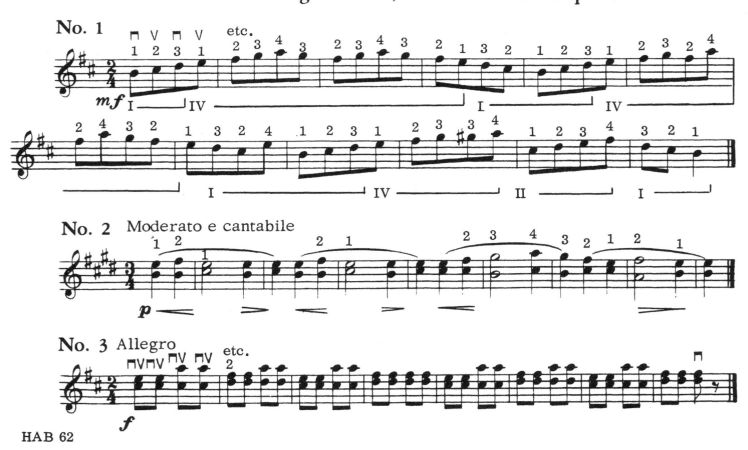

CHROMATIC SCALE

The chromatic scale, in contrast to the major and minor scales, is constructed entirely by half-steps. The most convenient fingering is 1-2-3-4.

38. SLOVAKIAN DANCE SONG

Con anima

39. THE THIN ROWAN TREE[1]

RUSSIAN FOLK-SONG

Con tristezza

1 Editor's note - The rowan tree is a Eurasian tree of the apple family. Sometimes the American mountain ash is called rowan.

2 Look up fermata in glossary.

CHAPTER X

PIECES IN THE RANGE OF FOUR POSITIONS

40. KRIZHACHOK

BYELORUSSIAN FOLK DANCE[1]

41. YOUNG BRIDE

RUSSIAN FOLK SONG
Arr. by N. FOMIN

Repeat from beginning to "Fine"

---

1 Byelorussian - White Russian - Ed.

40

42. GOLDEN TAIGA [1]

V. PUSHKOV

Moderato con emozione

43. AUTUMN LEAVES

B. MOKROUSSOV

Tempo di Valse, lento

[1] Vast Siberian forest.

HAB 62

44. BARCAROLA
"Guitar Sounds Are Heard on the River"

A. NOVIKOV

HAB 62

45. WHERE IS MY GARDEN?

V. SOLOVIEV-SEDOY

Moderato con emozione

Complete sound-range of Balalaika with 19 frets

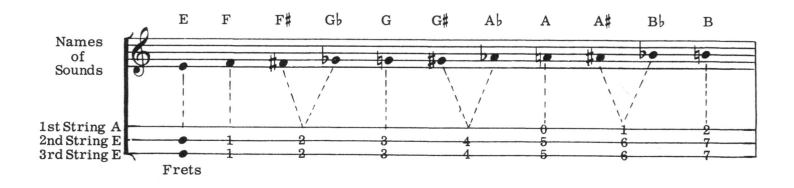

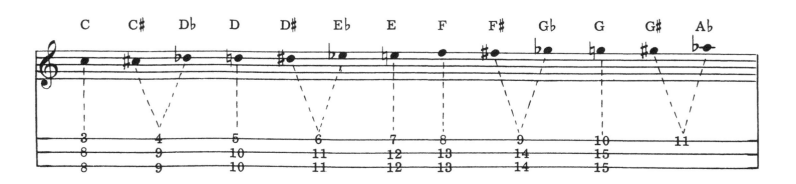

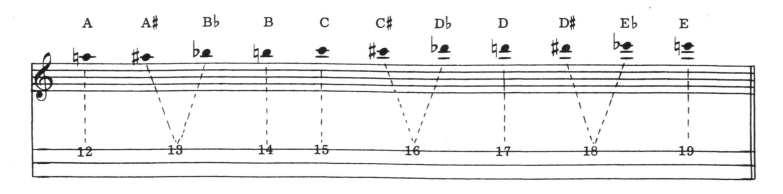

HAB 62

PART IV - SUPPLEMENT

FIFTH, SIXTH, SEVENTH AND EIGHTH POSITIONS

46. LULLABY

Moderato con sentimento

T. KHRENNIKOV

ritardando

47. VOLGA MELODIES

Moderato con gioia

Y. SHCHETKOV

48. THERE ARE MANY PATHS IN THE FIELD

RUSSIAN SLOW FOLK SONG
Arr. by N. FOMIN

Adagio con sentimento

49. OH, YE MISTS...

VL. ZAKHAROV

Calmato con decisione

HAB 62

46

50. OVER THE GREEN MEADOW

A. NOVIKOV

51. HOME SICKNESS

D. SHOSTAKOVICH

HAB 62

52. LIMERICK

Moderato

I. DUNAYEVSKY

53. DO NOT CRY, LITTLE QUAIL

Moderato, cantabile

F. MASLOV

48

54. URAL COMEDY SONG

Allegretto, energico

L. LIADOVA

55. URAL ROWAN TREE

E. RODIGIN

Moderato, cantabile

HAB 62

56. MOSCOW'S WINDOWS

T. KHRENNIKOV

Quasi moderato cantabile

57. MOSCOW EVENINGS

V. SOLOVIOV-SEDOY

Moderato, cantabile

58. ALL ROADS ARE OPEN TO US

A. OSTROVSKY

Moderato tempo di Valse

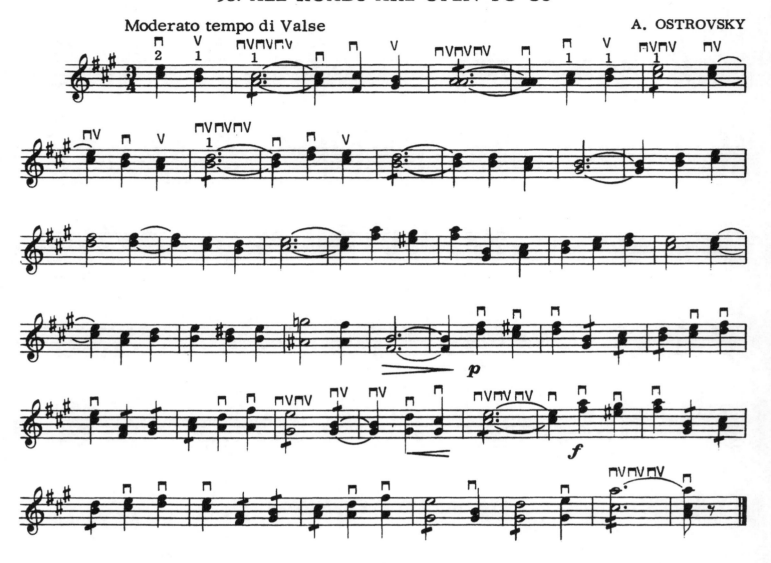

59. SAD WILLOW TREES

M. BLANTER

Adagio

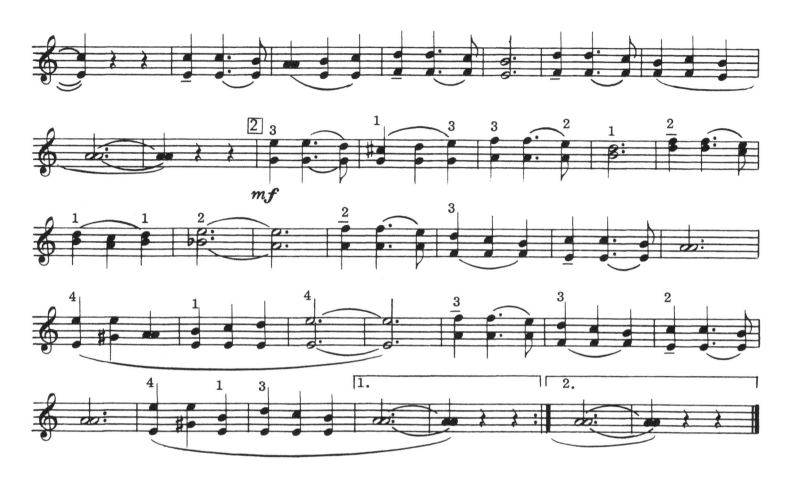

60. OUR COUNTRY

Cantabile con moto

D. KABALEVSKY

The fingering and manners of playing this piece are left to the student.

61. SHE SAID NOTHING

V. SOLOVIOV-SEDOY

62. HOW NICE IT IS ALL AROUND

I. DUNAYEVSKY

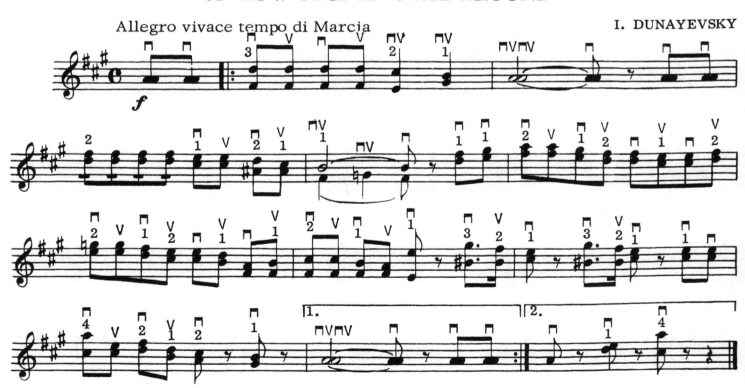

63. MOSCOW WALTZ

M. BLANTER

64. THE BERRY

RUSSIAN FOLK DRINKING SONG
Arr. by B. TROYANOVSKY

Adagietto e grandioso

65. SCENE FROM A BALLET

V. ANDREYEV

In "Scene From a Ballet" appear figurations $\begin{smallmatrix}3\\ \end{smallmatrix}$ called triplets. These three triplet eighth notes are played in the time of one beat. Triplets are executed down-up-down.

Tempo di Mazurka

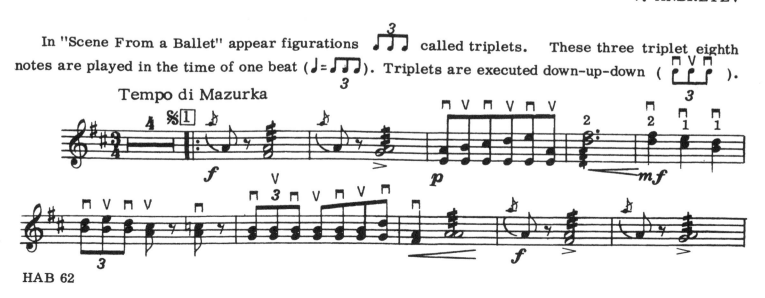

56

ritardando

Fine

Trio calmato

HAB 62

Repeat from 𝄋 to Fine

66. THE DNIEPER ROARS AND MOANS

UKRAINIAN FOLK SONG

67. I MET YOU

Romance

I. KOZLOVSKY
Taken down from the
voice of I. Moskvin

58

Glossary of musical terms

A – Letter name of one of the seven basic tones. The first string of the balalaika is tuned to A of the first octave (a').

Accelerando (accel.) – A playing direction indicating gradual speeding up of the tempo.

Accent – Strong emphasis of a note, indicated by > over the note.

Accidental – A symbol indicating alteration of a basic tone. A sharp (♯) raises a note a half-step. A flat (♭) lowers it a half-step. A natural (♮) cancels a preceding sharp or flat. A double sharp (x) or double flat (♭♭) alters a note by two half-steps (a whole-step).

Arpeggiato, arpeggio – Literally, in harp style. A manner of playing in which the notes of a chord are sounded successively (instead of simultaneously), indicated by a wavy line (⦃) before the notes of the chord. Arpeggiato is performed by the right thumb.

A tempo – A playing direction following rit., rall. or accel. indicating return to the former speed (tempo) of the composition.

Bar – A vertical line across the staff (also known as bar-line) dividing music into measures (also known as bars). See measure.

Bayan – An accordion-like instrument with buttons for the right hand rather than a piano keyboard.

Beam – Horizontal or slanted line or lines connecting several notes

as in

Body – Of a stringed instrument, the largest part — the sound chamber. The body of a balalaika is triangular in shape.

Bridge – A wooden support which keeps the strings of an instrument raised over the soundboard and fingerboard.

Caesura – Symbol (ν) indicating a barely noticeable stop between musical phrases, comparable to a quick breath (luftpause).

Chord – Simultaneous sounding of three or more notes of different pitch.

Clef – Sign used on staff to indicate pitch of notes on lines and in spaces. The G clef (treble or violin clef) 𝄞 is used for balalaika music. The F clef (bass clef) 𝄢 is used for lower pitched music.

Crescendo – Increase in the intensity (volume) of a tone, indicated by ◁ or cresc.

Da capo (D. C.) – Repeat music from the beginning.

Dal segno (D. S.) – Repeat music from the sign 𝄋.

Decrescendo – Gradual decrease in intensity (volume), indicated by ▷ or dim.

Domra – Russian stringed instrument of the lute family played by plucking. The domra usually has three strings tuned in fourths (see interval), but sometimes has four strings tuned in fifths like a mandolin or violin. Since the end of the 19th century the domra has been perfected by V. Andreyev and introduced into domra-balalaika orchestras.

Duration – One of the four physical properties of a musical tone, the length of time a sound is sustained. Duration of sound is indicated by the form of notes. Durations of silence is indicated by corresponding rests.

	Notes	Rests	Number of beats
Whole	o	▬	4
Half	♩	▬	2
Quarter	♩	𝄽	1
Eighth	♪	𝄾	1/2
Sixteenth	♬	𝄿	1/4
Dotted quarter	♩.	𝄽· or 𝄽𝄾	1-1/2

HAB 62

Dynamic shading – Relative loudness or softness of music, indicated as follows:

ff	*fortissimo*	*very loud*
f	*forte*	*loud*
mf	*mezzo forte*	*medium loud*
mp	*mezzo piano*	*medium soft*
p	*piano*	*soft*
pp	*pianissimo*	*very soft*

E – Letter name of one of seven basic musical tones. The second and third strings of the balalaika are tuned to E of the first octave (e′).

Fermata – A musical sign (⌢• or ◡) indicating that a note or rest is to be given more than its normal duration. Also called <u>hold</u>. When a fermata appears over a double bar it indicates the end of the composition.

Fine – End of composition, used in connection with a partial repeat indication, such as da capo (D. C.) or dal segno (D. S. or 𝄋).

Fingerboard – The part of a stringed instrument against which the fingers press the strings to vary the pitch.

Flageolet tones – Flute-like tones (also called harmonics) produced on a stringed instrument by touching a string lightly at one of several particular places on the fingerboard (for instance, the 12th or 19th fret). Flageolet tones are indicated by small circles above the notes:

Flat – ♭ See <u>accidental</u>.

Forte (*f*), fortissimo (*ff*) – See <u>dynamic shading</u>.

Friser – See <u>roll</u>.

Glissando – Literally, gliding. A sliding effect (up or down) produced by sliding the fingers of the left hand along the string(s). It is indicated by 〰〰 〰〰 or *gliss*.

Half-step – The smallest interval between adjacent musical tones in our system. For instance, between B and C, E and F, G and G♯, A and B♭. (Also called <u>half-tone</u> or <u>semitone</u>).

Incomplete measure (or bar) – An irregular first measure containing fewer beats than the number indicated by the time signature. It is usually balanced at the end by an incomplete measure containing only the missing beats.

Interval – The distance between two tones expressed in terms of the number of degrees (letter names) involved, including both tones.

C – C	unison or prime	C – G	fifth
C – D	second	C – A	sixth
C – E	third	C – B	seventh
C – F	fourth	C – C	octave

Intervals are further classified as perfect, major, minor, augmented or diminished according to how many half-steps they contain. (Refer to an elementary harmony or theory method for further information.) Two tones sounding in succession comprise a <u>melodic interval</u>. Two tones sounding simultaneously make a <u>harmonic interval</u>.

Key – A system of tones in relation to one of them (the keynote). See <u>scale</u>.

Key signature – Group of sharps or flats on staff at beginning of composition or movement. The key signature affects all notes so indicated until further notice.

Ledger lines - Short lines added above or below the staff to increase its range.

Legato - Smooth and connected, with no breaks between successive tones, indicated by a slur:

Mandolin - An Italian folk instrument played by plucking. It is tuned like a violin and has metal frets like a balalaika or guitar.

Measure - Segment of music included between bars (bar-lines) containing amount of durations (in notes or rests) indicated by the time signature. The first beat of the measure is the strongest.

Manner of playing - One of the various ways of using the right hand to produce sound from the strings of a balalaika. For example, strumming, tremolo, plucking, double-plucking, arpeggiato, friser.

Mode - Today, one of the characteristic flavors of a piece or movement, usually described as major mode or minor mode. ("In the Field a Birch Tree Stood" on page 16 is in the minor mode. "Visit Me, My Friend", on the next page, is in major mode.) There were seven ancient modes, represented by one octave of the major scale starting from each of the seven degrees. The natural minor scale is equivalent to the mode starting on the sixth degree. This and other modes are heard rarely, mostly in folk music.

Natural - ♮ See accidental.

Note - Symbol indicating pitch (by location on staff) and duration (by its form) of a tone (musical sound).

Nuance - Subtle variation in tempo, tone-color, or especially of intensity in performance. See dynamic shading.

Peg - Part of a balalaika or other stringed instrument which can be turned to tighten (or loosen) string to a desired tuning.

Phrase - As in spoken language, a sense unit composed of smaller units (motifs, or motives, of several notes each, corresponding to words). Two or more phrases, similar or contrasting according to the composer's intent, may make up a musical sentence or period.

Pizzicato (pizz.) - Manner of playing a stringed instrument by plucking a string with the thumb or a finger.

Plucking - Manner of playing a stringed instrument. Single pluck - stroking a string with right thumb or index finger. Double pluck - evenly alternating strokes, down (∨) by the right thumb (T) and up (⊓) by the right index finger (I).

Position - Placement of the fingers of the left hand on the fingerboard of a stringed instrument.

Repeat - Repeat signs ‖: :‖ indicate that music between the signs is to be played twice except for any music included within a repeat ending |1. which is to be played only the time indicated (first in this example).

Reprise - A repetition. See repeat.

Rhythm - Time element of music; the grouping of notes into beats, beats into measures, measures into phrases, etc.; the recurrence of pulses, patterns or similar figurations, giving a feeling to the listener of onward motion.

Ritardando (rit.) - A playing direction indicating slowing down of the tempo.

Ritenuto (rit.) - See ritardando.

Roll - A manner of playing the balalaika, in which the strings are stroked downward by the fingers of the right hand in turn. The small roll is executed by the fingers of the right hand, beginning with the little finger, without the use of the thumb. The large roll is accomplished by the fingers of the right hand, starting with the little finger and ending with the thumb in the manner of arpeggiato. (All rolls are executed briskly.) Also called friser. Indication: Fr

Rosette - Decoration around sound hole of balalaika.

Scale - Literally, "ladder of tones". A series of tones of rising pitch within one octave, related in a definite system of intervals. The principal scales are major, minor (natural minor, melodic minor and harmonic minor) and chromatic.

(The structure of these various scales is clearly shown on pages 29, 30 and 38)

Slur - A curved line, ⌒ or ⌣ .

Sound - The sensation of vibration as perceived by the organ of hearing. See tone.

Soundboard - A flat pine-wood board of 2 to 2.5 mm. thickness (about 1/16") covering the front (top) of the balalaika body.

Staff (or stave) - A system of five parallel lines on which notes are written to indicate pitch. Notes can be written on the lines or in the spaces between the lines. The staff can be extended by means of ledger lines. Lines of the staff are counted from the bottom up.

Stem - The vertical line of a note (♩ ♪).

Strumming - A manner of playing the balalaika, consisting of even continuous down and up strokes by the index finger of the right hand, with the wrist perfectly relaxed.

Tempo - Speed at which a musical composition is performed. The tempo may be indicated precisely, as by a metronome marking of so many beats a minute (♩ = 160), or loosely: Allegro (fast), Largo (slow). See also a tempo.

Timbre - Tone color; particular characteristics of tone of each instrument (or voice), often spoken of as bright, dull, etc.

Time signature - Group of numbers written within the staff at the beginning of a composition, or movement, such as $\frac{2}{4}$ $\frac{3}{4}$ $\frac{4}{4}$. The upper numeral indicates the number of beats in a measure (bar) and the lower one what kind of note gets one beat. (4 indicates a quarter note, ♩).

Time value - See duration.

Tone - A musical sound. Basic attributes of any tone are pitch, duration, intensity (volume) and timbre (tone color). Also, same as step, a musical interval.

Touch - A refinement of tone production or execution for expressive purposes: staccato (short, detached), legato (smoothly connected), accented, etc.

Tremolo - One of the basic manners of playing the balalaika. Fast down and up continuous motion of the right wrist while the fingers stroke the strings gives the impression of continuous sound. Tremolo is indicated by short lines (usually slanted) crossing the stem of a note (above or below a whole note).

Vibrato - Effect obtained on a stringed instrument by rapid pulsating of the finger on the sounding string below the bridge.

Virtuoso - A performer with masterly command of an instrument.

Virtuosi (plural) of the balalaika include V. V. Andreyev, B. S. Troyanovsky and N. P. Ossipov.

Whole-step - Musical interval of two half-steps.

INDEX OF MUSICAL PIECES

INDEX OF MUSICAL PIECES (Cont'd.)